The Power of the 50s

The Power of the 50s

by John Vaughan

Oxford Publishing Co

Frontispiece:—

Plate 1: The rotting timbers of Lostwithiel goods shed make an interesting frame for No. 50 037 *Illustrious* on a London bound express, and also afford the photographer some protection from inclement weather. This is still a very busy junction with several china clay trains per day using the line to Carne Point to unload at Fowey docks.

John Vaughan

Plate 2: A chance meeting on Hemerdon bank. At precisely 19.15 on the evening of 15th June, 1978 No. 50 047 *Swiftsure* running at about 70 mph on the 15.30 from Paddington meets No. 50 044 *Exeter* on the up milk climbing at less than 30 mph. It is clear from the exhaust which is making the greater effort at this point.

John Vaughan

SBN 86093 060 2

Printed by B.H. Blackwell in the City of Oxford

Published by
Oxford Publishing Co Ltd
8 The Roundway
Headington, Oxford.

INTRODUCTION

It is difficult to believe that, except for the High Speed Train 'power cars', the class 50 locomotives will probably be the last diesel express passenger locomotives built for British Railways. Their 16 cylinder English Electric diesel engines have powered diesel locomotives in this country for over 30 years, and were still being developed at the time the class 50s were built. The English Electric (now G.E.C. Traction Ltd.) 16 CSVT engine first appeared in 1600 hp form shortly after the second world war in a pair of LMS diesel locomotives. Four years later two Southern Region diesels were built at Ashford with the engine rated at 1750 hp. Finally in 1954 No. 10203 appeared with the 16 cylinder engine pushing out a commendable 2000 hp. This was to prove the forerunner of the class 40s — regarded by many as BR's first series production main line diesel. By 1962 the engine was producing 2700 hp and was installed in the DP2 prototype and subsequently the class 50s.

The DP2 prototype was the predecessor of the class and in addition to the power unit had identical bogies and traction motors. The prototype was enormously successful and in 15 months covered 200,000 miles breaking all previous mileage records. At one stage it was covering no less than 5,270 miles per week on the Eastern Region. Furthermore the running costs were only about one third of the complex Deltic locomotives. Sadly the prototype was destroyed in an accident during July 1967.

To provide high performance on the London Midland Region during the interim period prior to electrification BR ordered 50 English Electric 'D400' class locomotives which were built during 1967 and 1968 at the Vulcan Foundry at Newton le Willows. The locos were unique in being the first to be leased to BR by a manufacturer, with certain built-in guarantees regarding availability. On expiry of the lease some 10 years after contracts were signed all locomotives were purchased by BR for use on the Western Region.

In production substantial changes were made to the prototype and basically sound designs were modified. Rather than the 'Deltic' shaped body the class 50s were based on BR design panel lines with two piece windscreens and train identity headcode boxes. Also several sophisticated devices were fitted, many of which were rarely used (such as the 3 mph 'merry-go-round' slow speed running gear) and these modifications were to be detrimental to the overall reliability of the machines, with availability suffering as a result.

Nevertheless the class 50s transformed the main line service on the LM Region north of Crewe as they set the tracks alight with speeds of up to 110 mph being recorded on Anglo-Scottish expresses. Although the first two locos to be delivered were fitted with 'jumpers' permitting working in tandem, later examples were wired for multiple working but had plates over the controls. They were converted to work in multiple only after the LM announced that the machines were to work in pairs on accelerated timings introduced in 1970.

For certain services class 50s were rostered to work in tandem and with 5400 hp available the performance was staggering. The famous banks of Shap and Beattock were flattened overnight with speeds of over 80 mph over the respective summits. In fact the subsequent 25 Kv electric locomotives are, even today, only marginally superior to performance terms.

With the introduction of the overhead electric system the class was gradually displaced and transferred to the Western Region to replace an ageing fleet of diesel-hydraulic locomotives, which were incapable of providing electrical train heating for air conditioned stock. They were prime candidates for the job as Mark 2D coaches were being introduced on the London to Bristol services. Eventually all 50 engines were transferred and by 1975 they had penetrated the West Country as Laira crews received driver training.

Initially reliability suffered on the Western as crews and fitters became accustomed to their new mounts. However after the development and modification of some aspects of basic design satisfactory availability figures were obtained. It must be borne in mind that whilst in reliability terms locos such as the English Electric class 37 are their superior, the class 50s are covering twice the annual mileage, at twice the average speed.

Originally the class were overhauled by BR's Crewe Works but this work has now been transferred entirely to Doncaster. Major overhauls are completed every 4 years. Laira depot at Plymouth, which has an allocation of 45 class 50s, is equipped to deal with all repairs except for complete engine removal. The class 50s have always appeared in BR blue and yellow livery although many detail changes have occurred, especially in the position of the BR arrow symbols.

Perhaps the most significant development for the railway enthusiast was in 1977 when the newly appointed Chairman of BR, Mr (now Sir) Peter Parker, announced a change in policy regarding the naming of engines. During 1978 all 50 locomotives received alloy nameplates with red backgrounds. In the best traditions of the old GWR and WR of BR the names were to be those of famous warships past and present. It was stated that the class would be known as the 'Warship' class but the announcement was made far too soon after the demise of the class 42/3 'Warship' diesel hydraulics and the class are popularly known as 'Hoovers' or just plain '50s'. The 'hoover' sound is made by the cooling fan mechanism.

There is no doubt that the class has a following which is ever increasing. The locos are comparatively few in number and they now carry nameplates. Their sound is distinctive and when on full power they are impressive. It does seem ironic that, after replacing the 'Western' diesel hydraulics on first the Bristol route and then the West Country services, they themselves will be replaced on both routes by High Speed Train sets. In due course Inter City 125 trains will be running on inter-regional services and although the class 50s will undoubtedly replace the steam heat only 'Peak' class 46s in the early 1980s their ultimate destiny is unknown. Certainly these 100 mph machines will be with us for some time.

It has given me considerable pleasure to prepare this OPC publication and I have attempted to secure photographic material showing the class on every Region of BR. I would like to record my thanks to all my photographer colleagues for contributing, especially Brian Morrison and Dr John Cooper-Smith. Thanks are also due to Mike Woodhouse of Laira, Colin Marsden, G.E.C. Traction Ltd and to my publishers for the freedom afforded to me in selecting and arranging the contents of 'Power of the 50s'.

John A M Vaughan
Dorking 1978

Plate 3: No. 50 005 *Collingwood* on the up Paddington parcels in the Glynn Valley of the River Fowey climbs past the Mount turn-off on 2 April, 1979.

John Vaughan

Prototype DP2 Class 50

Plate 4: DP2 had the same body styling as the English Electric Deltic class 55 locomotives but due to the demands for a different cab layout and for a multiple working capability the production class 50s owe their appearance to BR Design Panel considerations. DP2 was not the first locomotive to carry the 16 cylinder engine. The origins date back to the immediate post war years when both the 10000/1 twins and three SR main line diesels used the 1600 hp 16 SVT engine. This was later used in class 40s in 2000 hp form before finally appearing as the 16 CSVT rated at 2700 hp.

courtesy G.E.C. Traction Ltd.

Plate 5: The English Electric prototype DP2 was introduced in May 1962 and to all intents and purposes was the forerunner of today's class 50s. The prototype was highly successful and within its first 16 months of service had covered 200,000 miles — at one stage averaging 5,270 miles a week for a six week period on the Eastern Region. DP2 is seen leaving Kings Cross for Edinburgh in 1963.

courtesy G.E.C. Traction Ltd

Plate 6: Class 50s under construction at the Vulcan Foundry, Newton le Willows in March 1968. All fifty locomotives were delivered in a little over one year, between October 1967 and the end of 1968.

courtesy G.E.C. Traction Ltd.

Construction

Ex Works

Plate 7: D400 ex works seen immediately after delivery. All locomotives were wired for multiple working, D400 and D401 were delivered with 'jumpers' to allow for working in multiple but other machines were converted at a later date. Outside the English Electric Vulcan Foundry a brand new D400 shows itself to the world in 1967.
courtesy G.E.C. Traction Ltd.

Plates 8, 9 & 10: No. D400 is seen here at Crewe after a visit to the paint shop and below are two views of jumperless class 50s showing each side of the loco-motive. No. D415 was photographed on 26th April, 1968 and No. D423 on 5th May, both at Crewe shortly after delivery.
All by Norman E. Preedy

Plate 11: An unusual picture of No. D400 leaving the Vulcan Works under its own power for the first time. The locomotive had a long pedigree having been conceived from the highly successful prototype DP2 and earlier English Electric designs.

courtesy G.E.C. Traction Ltd.

Plate 12: Later No. D400 was photographed outside the Vulcan Locomotive Works of English Electric (now G.E.C. Traction Ltd).

courtesy G.E.C. Traction Ltd.

Midland Region

Plate 13: One of the numerous vantage points for photographers between Grayrigg and Oxenholme is this cutting near the A685. Overshadowed by the distant fells is the 12.00 from Glasgow powered by Nos. 410 and 419 on 14th May, 1971.
John Cooper-Smith

Plate 14: In early days before being fitted with jumpers for multiple working on the Anglo-Scottish expresses No. D408 passes the Cowen Shildon engineering works at Carlisle with an up train.
Colin Marsden

Plate 15: Sunshine at Oxenholme as Nos. 404 and 415 head the up 'Royal Scot' on 14th May, 1971. It is alarming to see the train passing the signal at the 'on' position until the flagman is noticed by the signal post. A class 25 waits in the loop with a freight.
John Cooper-Smith

Plate 16: A 12 coach load for No. D405 seen here approaching Carlisle No. 12 signal box on 21st June, 1969 with an up train.
Colin Marsden

Plate 17: With the overhead catenary firmly in position for the West Coast Electrification No. 50 045 nears Shap with the down 'Midland Scot' on 2nd April, 1974.

Brian Morrison

Plate 18: The non-availability of two class 50s resulted in No. 405 coping single handed with the 16.00 Glasgow to Euston on 19th May, 1972. The train is seen passing Strickland, about 5 miles from Penrith.

John Cooper-Smith

Plate 19: Disturbing the peace at Lancaster are Nos. 436 and 442 on the 08.00 from Euston on a rainy 19th March, 1971.

John Cooper-Smith

Plate 20: Passing the site of the old watertroughs near Tebay are Nos. D403 and D427 on the 14.00 Euston to Glasgow. With introduction of the new timetable in May 1970 (using class 50s in tandem) over one hour was trimmed from the overall London to Glasgow journey time.　*John Cooper-Smith*

Plate 21: An impression of power and speed taken through a powerful lens (for safety reasons!) from a local Liverpool to Crewe EMU is this shot of class 50s on the main line between Winsford and Hartford in March 1971.

John Cooper-Smith

Plate 22: A pleasant study of the old Oxenholme station. With the splendid signal gantry, signal box and overall roof on the Windermere branch island platform in situ No. 411 leaves the station with a Carlisle to Euston train. No 411 was the third locomotive to be transferred to the Western Region in the early part of 1974.

John Cooper-Smith

Plate 25: It seems many years since one could associate Liverpool (Lime Street) with class 50s but this photo is a reminder of past workings and shows No. D447 arriving with the Liverpool portion of a Glasgow to Liverpool and Manchester train — the portions having been separated at Preston.

John Cooper-Smith

Plate 23: Crowds at Crewe station on 26th May, 1971 waiting for this up Blackpool train on platform 4. For years Crewe was (and for some lines still is) a major interchange point where diesel loco-motives were changed for electric ones and vice versa.

John Cooper-Smith

Plate 24: Passing the heavy industry around Warrington on 26th March, 1971 with the 14.00 Glasgow to Euston working are No. D412 and No. 419. During their time on the Midland Region all of the class 50s were allocated to Crewe shed and overhauled at Crewe Works.

John Cooper-Smith

Plate 26: The 12.50 Manchester Victoria to Edinburgh train passes Kearsley between Manchester and Bolton on 18 November, 1974. The loco is No. 50 036. The train will join up with a Liverpool portion at Preston before continuing northward.

D A Flitcroft

Plate 27: Man against nature as two unidentified class 50s ascend the hills with a Manchester to Glasgow train.

John Cooper-Smith

Plate 28: With the scar of the M6 motorway already appearing in the background but before the view was spoilt by overhead wires No. D432 seems to be winning the battle against the gradient at Shap Wells with an evening Manchester to Glasgow train, in May 1972.

John Cooper-Smith

Plate 29: With the forlorn sight of Carlisle Kingmoor in the background, some two years after the end of steam in the area, Nos. 415 and D448 head for the north with a down Anglo-Scottish express. The high speed, high mileage rosters on the LM Region caused the class 50 availability to fall to 70% and below for many months.

John Cooper-Smith

Paddington to Reading

Plate 30: A wide view of Paddington with HST class 253 units already outnumbering the class 50s on 9th August, 1977. From left to right the numbers are 253 018, 023, 027 and 50 027.

Brian Morrison

Plate 31: With the original livery of large BR symbols in opposite corners, subsequently superseded by firstly, a small symbol admidships and secondly, upon being named, by small symbols in opposite corners, No. 50 039 leaves Paddington with the 18.30 to Plymouth in May 1975.

Brian Morrison

Plate 32: An immaculate No. 50 032 prior to departure from Paddington with 1B73, the 14.30 to Paignton on 13th March, 1976. At this time the class 50 fleet was owned by English Electric and leased to BR but upon expiry of the lease all 50 locomotives were purchased by BR for a fraction of their current replacement value.

Norman E Preedy

Plate 33: Passing under the girder road bridges between Paddington and Royal Oak is No. 50 011 hauling the 17.12 down to Weston-super-Mare during May 1975.

Brian Morrison

Plate 34: During the last months of loco hauled operation a Bristol to London express passes Waltham St Lawrence at speed over welded rail on the up fast line. Although the maximum service speed of the class 50s is 100 mph speeds up to 110 mph have been recorded from time to time.

John Vaughan

Plate 35: The class 50 No. 50 018 is about to win the race against a class 47 on an Adex special at West Ealing as they both head for London. Note the missing section of track in the crossover in the foreground.

John Vaughan

Plate 36: A head-on view of class 50 at speed with a down express at Ruscombe.

John Vaughan

Plate 37: Another class 50 about to overhaul a train on an adjacent line is No. 50 031, although the opposition is hardly competitive, in the shape of class 31 No. 31 306 on an express parcels at Ruscombe just east of Twyford. The date is 24th June, 1978 and the class 50 is on an up train from Penzance.

John Vaughan

Plate 38: Nos. 50 040 and 50 017 double head the 12.00 Glasgow to Euston at Ais Gill on the Settle and Carlisle line on 14th April, 1974.
John Cooper-Smith

Plate 39: A Liverpool to Glasgow train on the evening of 9th September, 1972 is single headed as it climbs near Shap Wells beside the first evidence of the forthcoming electrification.
John Cooper-Smith

Plate 40: No. 50 021 in the snow covered hills around Ais Gill with a Manchester to Glasgow express in February 1974.
John Cooper-Smith

Plate 41: Descending from Shap summit at Greenholme is No. 50 010 with a special freight on 20th July, 1974.

Gavin Morrison

Plate 42: Snow at Horton in Ribblesdale as No. D419 passes with a down express on 29th November, 1969.

Gavin Morrison

Plate 43: Some class 50s were running on the Western Region under their original '400' series before the BR renumbering scheme was applied to all locos. No. 405 (now 50 005) was the sixth class 50 to be transferred to the Western Region in March 1974 and is seen here on the up 1A45 on 16th May, 1974 passing West Ealing.

Norman E Preedy

Plate 44: On the final stretch of track on its 202 mile journey the 09.55 from Paignton races through the suburbs at Southall behind No. 50 016 on the 23rd June, 1976.

Brian Morrison

Plate 45: A busy scene at Reading with No. 50 030 on an up parcels running through the centre road whilst No. 50 016 in charge of a down express passes a Southern Region 4 Cig unit which will return to Waterloo.

Norman E Preedy

Plate 46: In its original livery No. 50 034 passes Old Oak Common with a down Birmingham train. The rake of Mark 2B coaches appeared regularly on such trains from 1976 when they were displaced from the West of England services by air conditioned stock.

John Vaughan

Plate 47: Getting the 13.30 Paddington to Penzance under way and picking up speed through Acton Main Line is No. 50 014. In 1977 each of the class 50 engines covered an average of 104,000 miles and although this is far less than Deltic figures, 2000 miles per week is nearly twice that covered by the average class 37.

Brian Morrison

Plate 48: Southall once had a sizeable engine shed but the main railway installation is now a DMU depot for the Western Region's suburban fleet of ageing units. Showing a trail of exhaust No. 50 026 makes for Weston-super-Mare with the 16.15 from Paddington on 20th March, 1976.

Brian Morrison

Plate 49: A 1974 photograph of the up 'Cornish Riviera' passing Savernake signal box, junction of the old GWR Marlborough branch. At this time the class 50s had only just appeared on West of England trains.

John Vaughan

Plate 50: At speed near Charlton Mackrell with the 07.53 ex Paignton is No. 50 018 in August 1975. Train identity headcode panels then served a useful purpose.

John Vaughan

Plate 51: An immaculate No. 50 049 with 1B46 (11.45) Paddington to Bristol passing Twyford and entering Sonning Cutting in August 1974.

John Vaughan

Plate 52: A rare shot of a class 50 running on the Western Region as 401 (before renumbering and with large BR arrow symbol) passing Iver with a down Bristol train in 1974.

John Vaughan

Plate 53: No. 50 049 *Defiance* leaves the last of five tunnels at Dawlish with the 08.01 Paignton to Paddington on 20th June, 1978.

Colin Marsden

Plate 54: It is an amazing sight to see a 117 ton 100 mph express passenger engine on a train of four china clay wagons on an obscure branch line which is bound to be near the 4 chain curve capability (minimum) of the loco. Rolling off the Drinnick Mill line at Burngullow is No. 50 001 *Dreadnought* with up clays. In the foreground is the Cornish main line, with one of the tracks out of sight.

John Vaughan

Plate 55: The old Thornbury branch now terminates at Tytherington Quarry where the nation's demands for road stone are partially satisfied. Deputizing for the more usual class 46 or 47 on 30th March, 1978 was No. 50 039, pictured here underneath the loading chutes.

Graham Scott-Lowe

Branch Lines

Plate 56: Regular class 50 runs on branch lines occur on summer Saturdays when branches boast through trains to or from London and the North. Newquay is one such example and this photograph shows No. 50 024 running out of the terminus and past the signal box in readiness to take its return working forward.

John Vaughan

Mixed Traffic

Plate 57: A 'sha
brake van and a
dozen 'dogfish'
hopper wagons
head westward
near Cheston in
the South Devo
hills with Brent
at 1019 feet
standing out in
distance. The lo
is No. 50 036
Victorious.
    John Vaugh

Plate 58: An
unusual load for
class 50. New ra
on concrete
sleepers burst ir
the sunshine fro
Somerton tunne
on their way fro
Taunton to Cas
Cary in readines
for Sunday trac
working. Runnir
under speed
restriction
conditions is No
50 014 in June
1978.
    John Vaugh

Plate 59: Bringing home the clay empties from the Potteries around Stoke-on-Trent is No. 50 040. With over 40 wagons behind her the loco starts the long descent to Exeter from Whiteball summit.
John Vaughan

Plate 60: A load of china clay from St Blazey yard to Carne Point, Fowey rolls into Lostwithiel with No. 50 009 *Conqueror* providing the main brake force. The loco will then take the up milk forward whilst a class 25 or 37 will run the clay down the side of the Fowey estuary.
Colin Marsden

Plate 61: Tunnel Exit 1. Somerton tunnel is, surprisingly, the nearest to London on the 'cut off' Berks and Hants route even though some 127 miles from Paddington. No. 50 048 *Dauntless* hauls the 06.15 from Penzance on 20th May, 1978. The engine failed later in the day whilst working the return 13.30 down near Witham.

John Vaughan

Plate 62: A class 50 working flat out is a memorable sight when viewed at close quarters. Certainly No. 50 001 *Dreadnought* was trying hard as it left Whiteball tunnel with the usual set of Mark 2D/E/F coaches on the 10.30 London to Paignton.

John Vaughan

Viaducts

Plate 63: The Fowey valley in Cornwall is heavily wooded and in the summer months access to some vantage points is obscured for the photographer by Forestry Commission plantations. With the aid of a telephoto lens No. 50 016 *Barham* was photographed on Clinnick viaduct with the early morning Penzance to Liverpool train.

John Vaughan

Plate 64: Derrycombe is a masonry viaduct in the heart of the Fowey valley in Cornwall. This is one of eight viaducts encountered in nine miles of track between Bodmin Road and Liskeard. At the head of the 07.48 Penzance to Liverpool, comprised of Mark 2B stock, is No. 50 045 *Achilles* on 13th June, 1978.

John Vaughan

Plate 65: On a delightful June evening a named class 50 crosses the 150 foot high Moorswater viaduct near Liskeard with the 18.25 Penzance to Paddington train. The original piers of Brunel's earlier structure can be seen between the arches. The present viaduct dates back to 1880. *John Vaughan*

Plate 66: The 09.20 Liverpool (Lime Street) to Penzance express headed by class 50 No. 50 050 (formerly D400) crosses Coldrennick viaduct. When the line was doubled in the latter part of the last century the brickwork was extended on the original supports and metal girders replaced the timber trestles. *John Vaughan*

In Scotland

Plate 67: Super scenery in the hills and forests around Abington as the 5400 hp turned out by No. D443 and D437 move the 16.00 Glasgow to Euston southward at a smart pace on 5th June, 1970.

John Cooper-Smith

Class 50s appeared in Scotland regularly from 1968 until 1974. They worked all Anglo-Scottish services for several years with the main expresses being double-headed. Routes included Carlisle to Glasgow via both Carstairs and Kilmarnock, Freightliners to the Polmadie area of Glasgow and even the occasional sortie to Perth, Edinburgh and Inverness.

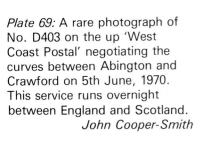

Plate 68: Hauling a long but partially loaded Freightliner train out of Polmadie, Glasgow on 9th September, 1971 is No. 409.

Norman E Preedy

Plate 69: A rare photograph of No. D403 on the up 'West Coast Postal' negotiating the curves between Abington and Crawford on 5th June, 1970. This service runs overnight between England and Scotland.

John Cooper-Smith

Plate 70: Pre-electrification super power makes short work of Beattock summit with Nos. D415 and D438 double-heading the 12.00 Glasgow to Euston express just south of Elvanfoot. The class 50s will continue to Crewe before an electric loco takes over for the final stage.
John Cooper-Smith

Plate 71: Taking a run at the bank No. D431 hurries through Beattock station with a Liverpool to Glasgow express in June 1970. A class 26 on a mineral train waits in the yard with a class 20 attached for banking purposes.
John Cooper-Smith

Plate 72: Meandering through the Drumlanrig Gorge in Dumfriesshire with the A76 trunk road in the background is No. 423 with a morning train from Glasgow to Birmingham during May 1972. Such secondary passenger trains were normally hauled by a single locomotive because for one thing, the timings were a little more generous than with the London expresses.

John Cooper-Smith

Reading to Westbury

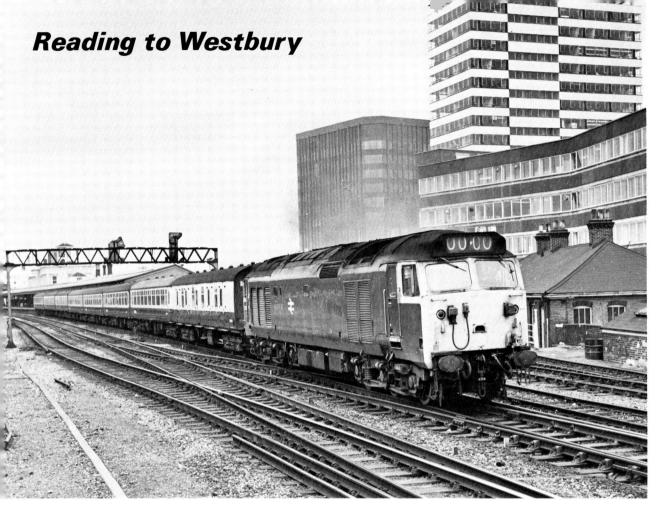

Plate 73: No. 50 021 leaves Reading with the 14.30 Paddington to Paignton on 7th April, 1976. The photo was taken about three months after BR abandoned the train identification codes and most headcode boxes showed '0000' before being covered over by spot indicators or headlights.

Brian Morrison

Plate 74: It is noticeable from the line of the coaches that the 09.30 ex Paddington has just cleared Savernake summit. The locomotive, No. 50 050 was not only the first member of its class to appear as D400 but the English Electric 16 cylinder 16 CSVT engine is that carried by the prototype DP2, albeit with a different crankcase.

John Vaughan

Plate 75: No. 50 023 approaches Hungerford Common with a down express in the early spring of 1976. Although dual braked the class 50s are fitted with electrical train heating equipment only and are rarely seen on steam heated stock in the winter months.
John Vaughan

Plate 76: In March 1977 No. 50 014 leaves Westbury for London with the 09.35 from Paignton. In the background is No. 47 170 on a Weymouth to Bristol train. The station was closed in September and October 1978 whilst Multi Aspect Signalling was installed and the track relaid.
Brian Morrison

Plate 77: The 11.55 Paignton to Paddington, 1A05, speeds towards Newbury with No. 50 026 in command on 23rd October, 1975. Less than a year later most trains to the West comprised air conditioned stock rather than the mainly Mark 2B set shown here. The concrete ducting on the down line is for cabling in connection with forthcoming Multi Aspect Signalling.

Philip D Hawkins

Plate 78: Split second timing by the photographer recorded class 50s passing each other at Newbury East on 27th January, 1978. In miserable weather No 50 024 on the down 14.35 Paddington to Paignton meets No. 50 016 on the up 'Cornish Riviera'. This entire area was converted from semaphore signalling to Multi Aspect Signalling in May 1978.

D E Canning

Plate 79: In the last months of manual signalling the 13.30 Paddington to Penzance express rushes through the well preserved Newbury Racecourse station. Raceday specials are still received on the relief roads and there is also an oil depot on the up side. No. 50 037 was in charge of the 10 bogie train.

John Vaughan

Plate 80: Awaiting the 'right away' at Newbury station on 4th October, 1976 was No. 50 009. After a fashion started during the last days of the class 52 'Westerns' some engines showed their running numbers (in four figure form) in the redundant train indicator panels prior to conversion. The train is the 15.00 from Penzance.

D E Canning

Plate 81: Past the peaceful setting of the Kennet and Avon No. 50 025, seen from an old canal overbridge just east of Crofton, speeds towards Reading with a train from Paignton.

John Vaughan

Plate 82: On a sunny day in May 1978 No. 50 026 *Indomitable* hurries the down 'Cornish Riviera' towards Crofton crossing. It always seemed unfortunate that sparkling new nameplates were applied to dirty locomotives but after a slow start they were applied so quickly that application could not coincide with the normal 6 week cleaning rotas.

▷

John Vaughan

Plate 83: After a snow fall in the severe winter of 1978/79 No. 50 04 *Ajax* rounds Crofton curve wit the 09.20 ex Paignton. Note that the BR arrow are still amidships despite the application of the nameplate. Also the telegraph posts have now been removed from this site following conversion to MAS signalling.
John Vaugha

Plate 84: In a very poor external condition and in need of a repaint No. 50 001 *Dreadnought* nears the village of Little Bedwyn with the 07.50 ex Paignton. To the right of the nameplate a crude patch of new pain covers the old BR arrows symbol which was in evidence prior to naming.
John Vaughar

Plate 85: A popular vantage point for lineside photographers is the road overbridge by the Wiltshire village of Little Bedwyn. The church clock shows evidence that the 09.30 ex Paignton has taken just 59 minutes to cover the first 65 miles of its journey, including a stop at Reading. No. 50 023 *Howe* provided the motive power.
John Vaughan

Plate 86: An interesting picture of No. 50 008 running high above the canal near Savernake signal box with the 07.50 Paignton to Paddington on 1st July, 1978. The BR symbol has been moved from the centre of the locomotive to the position below the cab side window in preparation for naming but the name has not actually been applied. The loco was allocated the name *Thunderer.*
John Vaughan

Plate 88: The 12.30 from Paddington is seen in the capable hands of No. 50 044 *Exeter* passing the site of the closed Savernake Low Level station. The station served the local community and was the junction for Marlborough, finally closing in April 1966. The chalk cutting visible in the background is the 'rival' Midland and South Western Junction Railway which closed during 1961 and boasted a Savernake High Level station.
John Vaughan

Plate 89: Making up for time lost in the West Country No. 50 037 uses all of its 2700 hp whilst heading the 09.10 from Falmouth to London between Woodborough and Pewsey.
John Vaugha

Plate 90: With immediate surroundings resembling a builders yard due to work on the MAS project Class 50 No. 50 016 *Barham* passes Woodborough signal box with the up 12.05 from Paignton on 27th May, 1978.
John Vaugha

Plate 91: Storming towards Woodborough at high speed is No. 50 030 *Repulse* on the 13.30 Paddington — Penzance. The signal was removed in January 1979. The locomotive was the last to carry the old four character headcode panel.

John Vaughan

Plate 92: Entering the racing ground in the Vale of Pewsey with a fairly short down Paignton train is No. 50 045 *Achilles*. On a summer Saturday in 1978 no down train stopped at Pewsey station between 09.44 and 17.53.

John Vaughan

Plate 94: A misty winter scene with a watery sun and frost on the ground is this view of Old Oak Common with No. 50 031 gently ticking over awaiting the next turn of duty.

Graham Scott-Lowe

Plate 93: The class 50 interloper has arrived at Laira, although it is a moot point as to whether it was class 50s, HSTs or BR policy which ousted the diesel hydraulics. Beside No. 50 026 are No. D1043 *Western Duke* and No. D1069 *Western Vanguard* on 13th September, 1975.

Philip D Hawkins

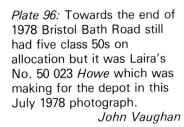

Plate 95: Stablemates at Long Rock make an interesting comparison of front end design with the distinctive 'Western' class diesel hydraulic on the left and the more standard 'corporate image' of the class 50 on the right. 7th July, 1976.

Brian Morrison

Plate 96: Towards the end of 1978 Bristol Bath Road still had five class 50s on allocation but it was Laira's No. 50 023 *Howe* which was making for the depot in this July 1978 photograph.

John Vaughan

Plate 97: It seems that the author and Brian Morrison spend at least part of their summer in Lostwithiel goods shed (see page 2)! However, this rare picture of an up parcels double headed by Nos. 50 017 *Royal Oak* and 50 027 *Lion* on 17th July, 1978 just had to be included in this section.

Brian Morrison

Plate 98: Double headed class 50s were a common sight when they were working the Anglo-Scottish expresses on the Midland Region but once transferred to the Western there was rarely need for trains to have 5400 hp at their head. Double heading on the Western was more likely to be for operational reasons. Awakening the peaceful atmosphere of Sonning Cutting with an up train from Bristol are this unidentified duo in March 1976.

John Vaughan

Western Region Double Headed

Plate 99: A sight and sound that will be remembered by the photographer for some time occurred on Sunday 11th June, 1978 when the 12.15 from Penzance to Paddington was double headed by Nos. 50 038 *Formidable* and 50 025 *Invincible*. The pair are starting their assault of the beautiful Fowey Valley by crossing Penadlake viaduct.
John Vaughan

Plate 100: Quietly situated in a valley 4 miles from Bodmin is Bodmin Road station. Being Sunday the signal box is switched out giving a long section from Lostwithiel to Largin. The passengers of the 10.15 ex Penzance are given a treat in the shape of No. 50 041 *Bulwark* double heading sister locomotive No. 50 002 *Superb* at least as far as Plymouth.

John Vaughan

Plate 101: It is always fascinating to see 100 mph express locomotives handling non passenger trains and one example of such workings are the traditional milk trains out of Cornwall. The returning empties run overnight and are rarely photographed. In the photograph opposite thirteen 3000 gallon milk tankers and three other vehicles cross the Tamar into Devon behind No. 50 044 *Exeter* at 18.51 on 15th June, 1978.

John Vaughan

Plate 102: After a slight signal check on the approach to Bodmin Road station No. 50 017 *Royal Oak* lifts a heavy milk train up the 1 in 66 past the home signal with the controller at notch 7 to cope with the long climb to Doublebois.

John Vaughan

Plate 103: The 16.10 St Erth to Acton milk is now booked for class 25 haulage as far as Lostwithiel where a class 47 or 50 takes over for the journey to the Capital. On a glorious day in a rather gloomy summer No. 50 010 *Monarch* accelerates towards Brownqueen tunnel with eleven six wheelers plus a parcel van or two including a splendid 'Siphon G', just visible in the photograph, taken on Sunday 11th June, 1978.

John Vaughan

Milk Trains

In London

Plate 104: At Ranelagh Bridge refuelling depot No. 50 017 *Royal Oak* awaits its next turn of duty whilst sister engine No. 50 016 *Barham* is refuelled from oil drums — a rather primitive arrangement.

Dr L A Nixon

Plate 105: A night study of No. 50 001 which was the second engine to be delivered as D401 at the end of 1967. The engine initially differed from later examples because in common with D400 it was fitted with jumpers for multiple working from the start. The loco had just arrived at Paddington with an up train.

Jeremy De Souza

On the Bath Road

Plate 106: An evening Bristol to London express speeds past Bathford in the lush countryside around Box behind an unidentified class 50.

Philip Fowler

Plate 107: Before the appearance of High Speed Trains the majority of Bristol and Weston-super-Mare to London trains were in the hands of class 50. They had taken over from the class 52 diesel hydraulics and to lesser extent the class 47s. Against a stormy sky No. 50 014 heads an up express from Bristol near Reading on 7th April, 1976.
Brian Morrison

Plate 108: On 24th June, 1976 the 11.47 Weston-super-Mare to Paddington train was hauled by No. 50 011 and was photographed passing Swindon Works. At this time the role of Swindon Works had changed dramatically from times gone by and more engines were being scrapped than built or repaired.
Brian Morrison

Plate 113: Passing St Anne's Park with the 10.15 from Paddington is No. 50 018. The photo was taken from the disused platform of the station which closed from the 5th January, 1970.

Graham Scott-Lowe

Plate 114: After withdrawal of class 50s from the London to Bristol expresses, after the High Speed Trains had become established, they headed few trains through Bath except when the Berks and Hants route was blocked. Such was the case in April 1978 when No. 50 016 Barham headed the 09.35 from Paddington into Twerton tunnel.

John Chalcroft

Bristol (Temple Meads)

Plate 115: Arriving at Bristol (Temple Meads) from the yards to form the 16.15 to London is No. 50 047 on 19th October, 1975.

Brian Morrison

Plate 116: Leaving a slight smoke screen across Bristol (Temple Meads) is No. 50 047 on empty stock bound for Malago Vale carriage sidings on 19th October, 1975.

Brian Morrison

Plate 117: Class 50s pass at Dr Day's Junction. On Sundays some West Country trains run via the Badminton route and Bristol. No. 50 001 *Dreadnought* pounds out of Bristol with the 09.30 from Plymouth whilst No. 50 025 slows the down 'Cornish Riviera' through the curves on the approach to Temple Meads.

John Chalcraft

Plate 118: A bird's eye view of Bristol (Temple Meads) sees No. 50 013 *Agincourt* on the 10.35 (Sunday only) Paddington to Plymouth heading westward on 24th June, 1978.

John Chalcraft

On the Southern Region

Plate 119: No. 50 036 stands at the buffer stops of Waterloo station after heading a railtour for 'real ale' enthusiasts up from Somerset. A Southern electro-diesel class 73 is on the right whilst behind a 4 VEP unit awaits departure.
Colin Marsden

Plate 120: A rare sight in the Southern Region's Victoria station was No. 50 044 which was the locomotive provided to haul a DAA/D&EG special to Weymouth on a Sunday in August 1978.
John Vaughan

Plate 121: During 1976/77 class 50s could be seen on the Southern Region regularly on the Acton to Norwood Junction freight. However, from the beginning of the new timetable in May 1978 the locomotive rostered was off an Oxford to Paddington morning commuter train and was therefore nearly always class 47 hauled. On 20th April, 1978 No. 50 040 passed Wandsworth Common.

Stanley Creer

Plate 122: Class 50 on the Southern's Central Division. No. 50 016 *Barham* pauses at Dorking North with an RPPR 'Southern Invader' tour on 7 April, 1979.

John Vaughan

Plate 123: An interesting working on most summer Saturdays was when the Derby to Weymouth holiday train worked forward from Bristol behind a class 50. On 12th August, 1978 No. 50 023 *Howe* was provided and is seen here at the buffer stops at the Weymouth Terminus.

John Vaughan

In the Snow

Plate 124A: Class 50s in the snow. After an overnight snowfall No. 50 013 runs down toward Fairwood Junction, Westbury with the 10.30 London to Plymouth on 17th January, 1978.
Graham Scott-Low

Plate 124B: One of the fiercest blizzards in living memory occurred overnight on the 18th/19th February, 1978 in most western counties, causing transport chaos. This scene at Exeter (St David's) on Monday 20th February shows a class 50 running into the station with an up train.
D E Canning

Plate 125: Running late in appalling conditions is No 50 028 with the 08.35 Penzance to Paddington near Whiteball on 18th February, 1978.
John Chalcra

Plate 126: High up on the Settle and Carlisle line a sprinkling of snow remains in the grass in April 1974 as No. 50 021 passes Ais Gill with a Manchester to Glasgow train.
John Cooper-Smith

Plate 127: A heavy snow shower in mid March starts to build up on the Triplex Safety Glass windscreen of No. 50 035 *Ark Royal* at Reading (on the 10.50 Paddington to Birmingham (New Street)) but fails to settle on a wet platform.
John Vaughan

Westbury to Exeter

Plate 128: A deep cutting in the heart of Somerton, Somerset sees No. 50 023 *Howe* running westward with the 12.23 Paddington to Paignton on 20th May, 1978. This engine was the last to be outshopped from Crewe before Doncaster took over the heavy maintenance of the class.
John Vaughan

Plate 129: The first class 50 to be named was No. 50 035 *Ark Royal* seen here running down to Clink Road near Frome with the 14.35 London to Plymouth semi fast.
John Vaughan

Plate 130: Fairwood Junction to the west of Westbury has always been a favourite spot for railway photographers because it is possible to see most trains running in an east or west direction. The lines in the foreground bypass Westbury whilst No. 50 002 *Superb* uses the lines through the station having stopped there with the 14.30 from Paddington to Paignton. The scene changed in September 1978 when MAS colour lights were introduced and one example can be seen in this photograph, turned inwards, beside the fifth bogie of the train.
John Vaughan

Plate 131: A stirring assault of the climb up to Whiteball is made by No. 50 038 *Formidable* as it thunders through Wellington with the fast 13.30 from Paddington to Penzance. The signals are controlled by the box visible above the last coach of the train.
John Vaughan

Plate 132: With signs of a stone train derailment remaining at Clink Road, with upturned wagons covered with tarpaulins, No. 50 034 passes swiftly by ahead of its eight Mark 1 first class coaches on the 07.45 Kensington to St Austell Motorail on 4th June, 1977.

Grenville R Hounsell

Plate 133: Through the cornfields near Cogload Junction in Somerset runs a class 50, coming off the Bristol Road with a down Liverpool to Plymouth inter-Regional express.

John Chalcraft

Plate 134: An unusual picture of a main line train taking to the single line through Frome station because of a derailment. Running from Blatchbridge Junction and into Frome with the 06.20 from Penzance is No. 50 022 on 18th April, 1977.

D E Canning

Plate 135: Winding through the curves in the attractive area around Somerton is an unidentified class 50 in April 1976. At that time class 50s shared the services to and from the West Country with the last thirty class 52 diesel hydraulics and a sprinkling of class 47s.
John Vaughan

Plate 136: Coming off the 'cut off', the direct line from London, at Cogload with the 16.35 Paddington to Plymouth is No. 50 025 *Invincible* on 12th August, 1978. The track over the girder bridge is the down Bristol line — see plate 133.
John Chalcraft

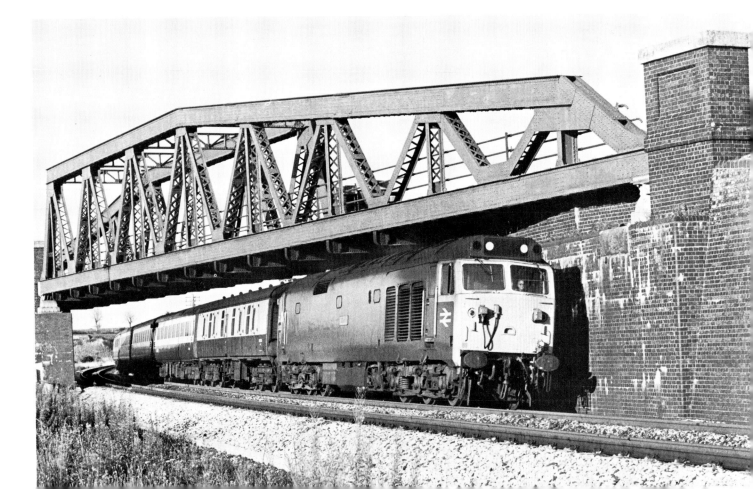

Plate 137: Whilst Westbury station was closed for three weeks in the late summer of 1978 for signalling and track modifications trains called at Frome where buses ran on to Westbury. This provided the usual sight of class 50s under the splendid overall roof. No. 50 031 *Hood* is seen here on the 07.30 from Paddington on 22nd September, 1978.

John Vaughan

Plate 138: Unusual power for the 14.40 (SO) Barnstaple to Paddington on 29th July, 1978 was No. 50 032 *Courageous* which was photographed from Blatchbridge Junction signal box.

John Chalcraft

Plate 139: A glimpse through the trees of No. 50 049 *Defiance* at speed on an up express passing a point near Wellington where some 74 years earlier *City of Truro* reputedly passed the 100 mph barrier for the first time in the United Kingdom.

John Vaughan

◁ Plate 140: A class 50 on Mark 1 coaches ascending the bank to Whiteball summit in the shape of No. 50 045 *Achilles* on the 11.10 Plymouth to Manchester inter-Regional train. Some have questioned the ability of the class to climb gradients well but this was answered in the early days when even single headed the 50s put up creditable performances over Shap and Beattock on the Midland Region.

John Vaughan

△ *Plate 141:* Powering the up 'Cornish Riviera' past the diminutive Whiteball signal box and into the tunnel is No. 50 048 *Dauntless* on 26th May, 1978. A tamping machine is stabled in the refuge siding.

John Vaughan

Plate 142: With the profusion of semaphore signals at Taunton (21 visible excluding ground discs in this photograph) it is difficult to believe that the photo was taken on 26th May, 1978. Furthermore the locomotive, No. 50 017 *Royal Oak*, on the 14.30 from Paddington, was the last of the fifty machines to retain the original livery with the very large BR arrows symbols. Note the heat haze from the engine.

John Vaughan

Plate 143: The name Tiverton Junction is a complete misnomer as the branch lines to Tiverton and Hemyock are now closed. However, the station retains much of its old atmosphere with manual signalling and old GWR station signs. In June 1978 No. 50 035 *Ark Royal* runs by with a down inter-Regional it had taken over at Birmingham.

John Vaughan

Plate 144: A pleasant study of the traditional view of Exeter (St David's) station. In need of a repaint is No. 50 028 at the head of the 12.23 from Paddington. The stock on the left is for London Waterloo via Salisbury.

Brian Morrison

Plate 146: Approaching Cowley Bridge Junction in the valley of the River Exe is No. 50 009 with 12 vehicles forming the 11.25 Plymouth to London on 21st July, 1977. Nearby the former LSWR north Devon lines leave the GWR route to Taunton.

Brian Morrison

Plate 145: Racing down from hills around Whiteball and through Tiverton Junction is No. 50 027 on a train from the Midlands. On the right are the remains of the old Culm Valley branch to Hemyock which closed to passengers in 1963 and completely in 1975. The M5 motorway completely severed the trackbed just to the east of the station. The oil depot behind the engine is supplied from Fawley and regularly receives class 33 hauled tanker trains.

Brian Morrison

Names and Namings

Plates 147, 148 & 149. Three plates carried by class 50s. The top photograph shows the standard nameplate fitted to all class 50s during 1978. When the entire fleet were leased to BR by English Electric all locomotives carried the plate seen here. On expiry of the lease BR purchased all 50 locos and most of the plates were removed. Below is the nameplate of the first class 50 to be named, *Ark Royal* together with the special plaque presented by the crew of the aircraft carrier HMS Ark Royal.

Brian Morrison

Plates 150 & 151: The second class 50 naming was at a ceremony at Reading on 16th March, 1978. In the top picture the white ensign is pulled to reveal the Swindon made nameplate. The loco was named by the Commanding Officer of HMS Dauntless (a training establishment) Chief Officer Jeayes who is standing beside the WR Divisional Manager. With the honourable lady in the second man's seat the loco then left the bay platform for a short run to Reading West. Needless to say the locomotive was turned out in immaculate condition.

John Vaughan

Class 50	
Weight tonnes	117
Brake force tonnes	59
ETH index	
RA	6
Max speed mph	100

Plate 152: A newly painted cabside plus the usual transfers on No. 50 002 at Crewe Works on 20th September, 1975.

L P Gater

Plate 153: In 1975 before the transfer of class 50 maintenance from Crewe Works to Doncaster No. 50 002, then allocated to Bristol Bath Road, stands in the diesel repair shop.

L P Gater

Plate 154: On a Crewe Works open day in September 1973 class 50 No. 436 (now 50 036) was receiving a general overhaul.

Richard Charlson

In the Workshops

Plate 155: No. 50 018 *Resolution* at Laira, photographed from the inspection pit where fluorescent lighting enables a 24 hour maintenance programme to be worked.

John Vaughan

Plate 156: Six locomotives can be accommodated in the Laira workshops at any one time. All repairs except engine removals can be done at the depot. The reason for this is the lifting capacity of the overhead crane (from where the photograph was taken) which could easily cope with the Maybach MD655/650 engines of the diesel hydraulics but not the vast 16 CSVT engine of the class 50s. 'Not to be moved' are Nos. 50 023 and 50 018 in front of two class 47s.

John Vaughan

Plate 159: Resting on metal stands minus bogies, traction motors and engine is No. 50 03 Furious in June 1978.

John Vaugha.

Plate 160: Don't look in your number books for '50 084'. The staff on Doncaster Works had something of a legpull with the loco spotters during their Doncaster 125 open day in June 1978 when a rogue transfer was applied over the '3' as seen in the picture below.

John Chalcraf

Plate 157: Gleaming in the Doncaster Works paint shop with paint pots in the foreground is No. 50 016 on 20th November, 1977.

L P Gater

Plate 158: Sandwiched between two class 37s at Doncaster Works whilst awaiting attention in the shops is No. 50 024 Vanguard.

John Vaughan

Exe to the Tamar

Plate 161: A favourite location for photographers is Aller Junction to the west of Newton Abbot, where the Paignton line diverges from the Plymouth line. On 21st August, 1976 No. 50 025 on the 12.26 Paddington to Paignton relief nears the junction with a load of holidaymakers bound for Torbay.

Norman E Preedy

Plate 162: The sea wall at Teignmouth on 8th August, 1975 saw No. 50 032 pulling away from the station with the 09.55 Paignton to Paddington. Note the original livery with the very large BR symbol and the tiny plate on the side of the engine which states that 'This loco-motive is the property of English Electric Leasings Limited'.

Brian Morrison

Plate 163: Up and down trains at Newton Abbot. No. 50 030 stands at the down platform whilst No. 50 016 approaches with an up train in July 1976.

Norman E. Preedy

Plate 164: With its customary train of eight Mark 1 first class coaches and eight car flats the 07.53 Kensington Olympia to St Austell Motorail train pounds through Aller Junction on full power to attack Dainton bank on 10th June, 1978 with an immaculate No. 50 037 *Illustrious* at its head.

John Vaughan

Plate 165: The glorious south Devon countryside is at its best on the fringe of Dartmoor around Brent. Passing the old signal box and station site is No. 50 049 *Defiance* on the 12.2? from Penzance to London. The station closed in autumn of 1964, about a year after the service from Brent to Kingsbridge was withdrawn.

John Vaughan

Plate 166: A magnificent site from the last winter of loco haulage on the famous 'Cornish Riviera' express sees No. 50 013 *Agincourt* catching the rays of the afternoon sun as the sound and exhaust from the four exhaust ports shatters the peace of the south Devon coastline near Teignmouth on 3 February, 1979.

John Vaughan

Plate 167: Finding a patch of sunshine on an otherwise cloudy day No. 50 017 *Royal Oak* rounds the curve into Brent with the down 'Riviera' on 15th June, 1978. Through the shrubbery behind the permanent way worker (right background) ran the old branch line to Kingsbridge which was closed in September 1963.

John Vaughan

Plate 168: An impressive view of the western exit from Dainton tunnel which shows clearly the steep descent from the summit which continues down to Totnes. Framed between the two semaphore signals the 13.30 Paddington to Penzance leaves the tunnel behind a rather grubby class 50.

John Vaughan

Plate 169: Severe curves and steep gradients on the approach to Rattery summit necessitate a 50 mph speed limit in the down direction and a 55 limit on the up road. Both speed restriction signs are visible in this picture of the inter-Regional 15.15 Plymouth to Liverpool powered by No. 50 019 *Ramilles.*
John Vaughan

Plate 170: One of the few remaining West Country to London trains comprising old Mark 1 rolling stock is the 10.38 (SO) Newquay to Paddington. With brakes hard on, the up Newquay on 10th June, 1978 passes Stoneycombe Quarry behind No. 50 022 *Anson.*
John Vaughan

Plate 171: A three minute early arrival at Plymouth for the 09.35 from London seen here passing the Plymouth Eye Infirmary to the east of North Road station behind No. 50 019 *Ramilles*. In the background the usual 08 shunter toys with a van. The train will continue to Penzance behind the same class 50 which will then have a short 46 minute rest before working the 16.07 up from Penzance.

John Vaughan

Plate 172: After a shower of rain No. 50 040 gets to grips with the 12.00 Plymouth to Paddington over the last few yards of Hemerdon bank. The bank presents a problem for most up trains for whilst they manage a 70 mph sprint past Laira depot, 2 miles at 1 in 41 slow most to between 25 and 30 mph at the summit.

John Vaughan

Plate 173: With the aid of a telephoto lens and strong back-lighting No. 50 002 *Superb* makes a fine sight leaving the Royal Albert Bridge over the River Tamar with the Penzance to Crewe parcels. The massive girders of the Tamar road bridge can be seen in the background.

John Vaughan

Plate 174: Having dropped three coaches plus buffet car at Plymouth the 09.30 from Paddington to Penzance nears St Budeaux on the outskirts of Plymouth with the remaining five coaches plus BG. The engine is No. 50 019 *Ramilles*. Note the substantial four arch girder bridge.

John Vaughan

Plate 175: Approaching Keyham to the west of Plymouth is No. 50 015 *Valiant* with the 16.07 Penzance to Paddington. Additional coaches and a buffet car will be attached at North Road station. The line joining the down main line is a siding which runs towards the old dockyard, although all of the former LSWR lines to Devonport have long been closed and lifted.

John Vaughan

Plate 176: After bringing its train into Paignton No. 50 020 continues with the empty stock (ECS) on to Goodrington sidings. The line on the right is the Torbay and Dartmouth railway line to Kingswear. Photographed on 11th July, 1976 during a period when headcodes reflected the strong feeling towards the withdrawal of the '1000 class' (class 52) engines.

Norman E Preedy

Plate 177: Passing Kingskerswell on the Torbay branch with the summer Saturdays 12.23 from Paddington is No. 50 045 *Achilles*. The formation is slightly unusual in that the BG used for luggage separates the second and third passenger coaches, rather than being next to the engine.

John Vaughan

The Paignton Branch

Plate 178: A shot from the overbridge of Paignton station before controlled barriers were installed. With the lower quadrant semaphore in the 'off' position No. 50 023 leaves for Newton Abbot on 4th August, 1975.

Brian Morrison

Plate 179: The 16.50 (FX) from Plymouth to Paignton on 6th August, 1975 arrives on time after reversal at Newton Abbot. The loco is No. 50 016 and the vehicle next to the engine is a dual heated BG with white metal bearing axle boxes of Midland Region origin. Paignton south signal box in the distance controls signals and the crossing for both BR and Torbay and Dartmouth trains.

Brian Morrison

Settle and Carlisle

Plate 180: The Settle and Carlisle is often used as a diversionary route and such was the case on a weekend in May 1974 when a pair of class 50s passed Ais Gill summit with a smart rake of Mark 2B coaches bound for London. The scene is overlooked by the 2324 feet of Wild Boar Fell.
John Cooper-Smith

Plate 181: A photographic stop at Garsdale for one of the first enthusiasts specials to use class 50 power was in the Spring of 1974. On a WRC tour which included a run from Crewe to Carlisle No. 50 023 stopped at Garsdale on Easter Monday.

Grenville R Hounsell

Plate 182: The classic Ribblehead viaduct photographed at a distance to show the scale of the structure. A double headed Euston to Glasgow train on Sunday 3rd June, 1970 heads north with Blea Moor in the distance.
John Cooper-Smith

Plate 183: An impressive study which typifies the scenery on the Settle and Carlisle line of the former Midland Railway. High on Arten Gill viaduct with an up fitted freight is No. 400, the first class 50 to enter traffic in October 1967, photographed on 18th September, 1972.

John Cooper-Smith

On the Eastern Region

Plate 185: A pleasant study of No. 50 041 at Bridge Junction, Doncaster on a works test train on 7th July, 1977. Class 50s occasionally travel to York and even to Newcastle on post-works test runs with empty stock.

Gavin Morrison

Plate 184: Fresh from overhaul at Doncaster Works No. 50 031 passes St James Bridge Junction having just returned from York with a 'running-in' test train on 19th May, 1978.

A R Kay

Plate 186: Another class 50 works test run was also in the hands of No. 50 041 which was photographed at Church Fenton a week later than in plate 185.
Gavin Morrison

Plate 187: On 9th June, 1978 the 09.20 Hull to Kings Cross failed near Goole and the only locomotive available to take it forward was No. 50 020. After arriving 45 minutes late the loco passes 'Deltic' class 55 No. 50 019 *Royal Highland Fusilier* before heading the 14.45 departure to Leeds. A rare working indeed.
Jeremy de Souza

Rare Locations

Plate 188: Crossing the River Thames on Chelsea bridge with the 10.55 Acton to Norwood freight is No. 50 024 on 25th May, 1977.

Brian Morrison

Plate 189: Heading light engine from Perth to Inverness to collect a Motorail train, No. 428 (the D prefix having been dropped) crosses class 24/2 No. 5126 at Pitlochry on 5th June, 1973.

Grenville R Hounsell

Plate 190: Class 50s have never been particularly common in South Wales but No. 50 027 strayed to Cardiff Canton in October 1977 and is seen here in the carriage sheds before working a special back to London.

John Chalcraft

Plate 191: Perhaps the most unusual class 50 location was secured in this picture of a Manchester United football supporters train crossing the Pennines on the Woodhead route near Torside on 14th March, 1970 powered by No. D414.

Gavin Morrison

Plate 192: For a few weeks during the spring of 1975 eight of the remaining Crewe based class 50s made appearances on the Trentham (Stoke) to Ironbridge 'merry-go-round' coal trains. Beside Wolverhampton's refuse incinerator No. 50 022 sets back onto the Bushbury Spur at Cannock Road Junction with empties on 8th April, 1975.

Geoffrey F Bannister

Plate 193: On the cross country line from Thingley Junction to Bradford Junctions passes the 15.30 (Sunday) Paddington to Penzance headed by No. 50 016 *Barham* near Melksham having been diverted via Chippenham, Trowbridge and Westbury.

John Chalcraft

Cross Country

Plate 194: In the heart of the Cotswolds No. 50 017 *Royal Oak* makes a vigorous climb towards Sapperton between Chalford and Frampton Mansell with the 15.06 Worcester to Paddington.

Graham Scott-Lowe

Plate 195: Bursting out of Bradford-on-Avon tunnel with the diverted 06.00 Plymouth to London is No. 50 029 on 29th April, 1978.

John Chalcraft

Plate 196: Formerly the preserve of class 45/46 'Peaks' English Electric class 50s are now rostered on some of the cross country and inter-Regional trains to or from Birmingham or Gloucester. No. 50 044 *Exeter* is seen here on the 13.20 Liverpool to Plymouth on 4th March, 1978 near Wickwar tunnel.

A R Kaye

Plate 197: Another headcode showing '1000' rather than 1E70 due both to the abandonment of train headcodes and in sympathy with the class 52s (1000 class) which were being withdrawn in July 1976 when this picture was taken. Rounding the curve into Gloucester with the Paignton to York train is No. 50 005.

Norman E Preedy

Plate 198: Passing Limpley Stoke in the Avon Valley is No. 50 028 on the diverted 09.45 from London to Bristol on 11th April, 1976. This route is used on most occasions when either the Badminton or Chippenham routes from Bristol to London are closed.

D E Canning

Plate 199: Changing from single to double track on the approach to Evesham station with an afternoon Paddington to Worcester (Shrub Hill) service is No. 50 034 on 19th September, 1977. Note the short lower quadrant signal in the foreground.

A R Kaye

Plate 200: Accelerating along the now single line at Pershore is No. 50 038 *Formidable* heading the 16.03 Worcester to Paddington. The area is famous for its fruit growing, especially plums.

John Vaughan

Plate 201: Catching the last rays of the evening sun the 15.43 Plymouth to Manchester speeds northward between Yate and Wickwar on 18th August, 1978 with No. 50 044 *Exeter* putting on a sprightly performance.

John Vaughan

Plate 202: Seen at Yeovil (Pen Mill) on the summer Saturdays only Weymouth to Derby service is No. 50 023 *Howe* which was waiting for a local DMU service from Bristol to arrive before receiving the token for the single line to Castle Cary.

John Vaughan

Plate 203: An interesting working which is occasionally class 50 hauled is the 07.55 from Paddington to Paddington via Banbury, Birmingham Worcester and Oxford. Having run down the Lickey incline No. 50 049 pulls into Bromsgrove station on 28th December 1977 where a handful of passengers are awaiting t join the train.

C R Dav

Western Region 50s on the London Midland Region

Plate 204: Having worked the 06.27 Plymouth to Liverpool (Lime Street) into Birmingham (New Street) No. 50 007 *Hercules* reverses into the centre road in readiness to return with the 12.20 back to the West Country. Appearances 'under the wires' are not unusual but the Midland are always anxious to return the machines to the Western as their drivers are not passed to drive them.

John Vaughan

Plate 205: Approaching Coventry with the 07.55 Paddington to Birmingham and then Worcester is No. 50 048 *Dauntless*. This train runs via Leamington Spa and Kenilworth and runs under the wires for over 19 miles into New Street.

Steve Turner

Plate 206: The first ever railtour to employ named class 50s was in March 1978 when a RPPR special ran from Paddington to Derby with Nos. 50 010 *Monarch* and 50 048 *Dauntless* running in multiple. The locos were named only two days before the trip. The pair were photographed at Luton.

Alan N Pierce

Plate 207: A Penzance to Paddington parcel train of 14 vehicles hurries past Cutmadoc hauled by No. 50 009 Conqueror.

John Vaugh.

Up Parcels and Perishables

Plate 208: Amongst the most interesting trains these days of standardisation are those conveying parcels and perishables. In this train powered by No. 50 048 Dauntless are BGs, CCTs, GUVs, and 4- and 8-wheel utility vans. The train is up from Penzance and is passing the site of Defiance Platform which closed to passengers from 27th October, 193 although a down loop was in existence until quite recently.

John Vaugha

Plate 209: An intriguing view of Penwithers Junction from high above the tunnel at Highertown, Truro. The up perishables hauled by No. 50 041 *Bulwark* is on the main line and the track disappearing into the distance is the Falmouth branch which still sees one through loco hauled train to Paddington on summer Saturdays — often class 50 hauled.

John Vaughan

Fifties in Cornwall

Plate 210: In very damp conditions No. 50 027 *Lion* passes Menheniot station with the morning 'up Liverpool'. The station retains its original buildings but the signal box on the left is closed as the line from Plymouth to Liskeard is all under the control of Plymouth panel.

John Vaughan

Plate 211: The 09.20 from Liverpool to Penzance rounds the curve into Par station with No. 50 014 *Warspite* pulling the rake of Mark 2B coaches past the semaphore home signals.

John Vaughan

Plate 212: Riding high 151 feet above the valley on St Pinnock viaduct was newly named No. 50 047 *Swiftsure* in June 1978 with the 08.38 up from Penzance. St Pinnock is the highest viaduct in Cornwall which in common with East Largin carries only single track. Singling took place in 1964 to save certain renewals and strengthening of the superstructure.

John Vaughan

Plate 213: Catching the rays of some welcome evening sunshine at Dobwalls No. 50 016 *Barham* lifts the Sunday 12.30 Paddington to Penzance via Bristol (Temple Meads) out of the East Looe Valley and up to Doublebois. The town of Liskeard can be seen in the distance across the rolling hills.

John Vaughan

Plate 214: A sheer delight is the old original wooden building on the up side of Lostwithiel station. The station was last painted just after the second world war and the chocolate and cream paint is looking dilapidated. However unlike the building on the down side which was demolished in 1976 a preservation order should save the remaining structure for posterity. No. 50 033 moves aloofly by on an up express.

John Vaughan

Plate 215: A splendid pastoral scene near Restormel Castle on Sunday 11th June, 1978 with No. 50 014 *Warspite* moving briskly by with the down 10.30 ex Paddington.

John Vaughan

Plate 216: Slowing for its Bodmin Road stop the 13.30 from Paddington running about 12 minutes late enters the station after its long descent of the Fowey Valley behind No. 50 033 *Glorious*. The curvature here is such that the up starting signal is located on the down side platform. New lamp standards seem a little incongruous when seen beside GWR station seats.
John Vaughan

Plate 217: A pleasing profile of No. 50 036 *Victorious* emphasises the 68 foot length of the locomotive as he runs down the delightful Fowey Valley and into Bodmin Road station on the Sunday 11.15 Plymouth to Penzance on 11th June, 1978.
John Vaughan

Plate 218: The old station of Burngullow closed back in 1931 but part of the station buildings and the signal box survive. The site is on the fringe of the vast china clay area around Hensbarrow and Longstone Downs and is still the junction for the Drinnick Mill mineral line. On full power with an up express is No. 50 048 *Dauntless.*

John Vaughan

Plate 219: Ageing rolling stock is allocated to the 13.59 Penzance to Birmingham (New Street) train seen here passing a multitude of flowering rhododendrons near Chacewater station with No. 50 025 *Invincible* up front on 12th June, 1978.

John Vaughan

Plate 220: Cornwall at its best. Taken from high on the hillside between Miltown and Lantyan No. 50 035 *Ark Royal* is in command of the 09.35 Paddington to Penzance as it pounds its way towards Treverran tunnel, seen through a high powered lens on 14th June, 1978. Par is the next stop.

John Vaughan

Plate 221: Passing the site of Marazion station, closed in October 1964, is No. 50 027 on the 13.55 Penzance to Bristol (Temple Meads) on 7th July, 1976. Of special interest are the camping coaches converted from old Pullman cars.

Brian Morrison

Plate 222: A general view of Par station showing not only No. 50 050 on the 14.58 Penzance to Paddington but the gradient to the west climbing towards St Austell, one of the first two class 37s introduced to the west country for the purpose of hauling china clay trains (just visible on the line to St Blazey and Newquay), and the vast china clay works on the horizon in the vicinity of Par Harbour.

Brian Morrison

Plate 223: With the bark of its 16 cylinders echoing against the hills surrounding Lostwithiel No. 50 035 *Ark Royal*, the flagship of the fleet, accelerates away from the station with one of the two direct trains to London which stop to pick up, the 16.07 from Penzance.
John Vaughan

Plate 224: Having slowed for the 40 mph permanent way slack at Gwinear Road No. 50 035 looks a proverbial powerhouse as she accelerates the down 'Cornish Riviera' express to the new line limit of 65 mph. *Ark Royal* is one of only two class 50s to be fitted with head-lights rather than the normal pair of translucent spots over the former train indicator.
John Vaughan

Plate 225: Passing Redruth with a down parcels/perishables (empties) is No. 50 007 *Hercules.*

Brian Morrison

Plate 226: Reversing into the motorail sidings at St Austell on 15th July, 1977 is class 50 No. 50 022. In recent times the Kensington to St Austell service has been class 50 hauled regularly, pausing at Reading and Newton Abbot to pick up and set down.

Brian Morrison

Plate 227: With yet another permutation of headcode on the indicator blind class 50 No. 50 010 heads westward between Scorrier and Redruth with the down 09.30 ex Paddington in July 1976.

Brian Morrison

Plate 228: Running down to Redruth from the area around Scorrier is No. 50 005 with the 08.40 Plymouth to Penzance on 15th July, 1977.
Brian Morrison

Plate 229: Whilst there is much evidence in Cornwall of the past industries of tin, lead, copper and arsenic mining it is difficult to incorporate the derelict remains of engine houses in a railway photograph. The best lineside example is the engine house of Hallenbeagle near Scorrier and No. 50 036 *Victorious* is seen passing the site with the 14.58 Penzance to Paddington.
John Vaughan

Plate 230: With excellent visibility on a sunny June day, Trink and Trecrom Hills, some 8 miles distant, and the villages of Copperhouse, Phillack and Carbis can be seen clearly. Making music amongst the hills is No. 50 049 *Defiance* on its way to Camborne with the 10.54 ex Penzance.
John Vaughan

Plate 231: Hayle station seems unusually busy in this photograph as the 12.37 departure for London enters the platform past the fine signal box. The box is normally switched out with signals in the 'off' position, unless a train is booked down to the Hayle Harbour line when the box is specially opened. The loco is No. 50 009 *Conqueror.*
John Vaughan

Plate 232: Rolling down towards Marazion in Mount's Bay on the last leg of its journey to Penzance is No. 50 038 *Formidable* on a down express from London on 16th June, 1978.

John Vaughan

Plate 233: Cornwall is noted for its viaducts and the somewhat inaccessible example at Angarrack is as impressive as any. Chased by a heavy patch of cloud No. 50 044 *Exeter* manages to stay in the sunshine as it nears Hayle with the first through train of the day from London, the 07.30.

John Vaughan

Plate 234: The 1V76 from Liverpool arrives at Penzance and was photographed from the signal box. The picture is unusual in that somebody seems to have twisted the jumper cable on the front of the engine. The beach on the right can be seen stretching away towards Long Rock.

Brian Morrison

Plate 236: A picture of 1B03, the 07.30 from Paddington, nearing St Erth (junction for St Ives), before the advent of air conditioned coaches on the route with No. 50 013 slowing for the station on 30th July, 1975.

Brian Morrison

Plate 237: No. 50 045 *Achilles* is framed by foliage as it starts the 08.05 ex Bristol from Hayle station and onto the viaduct over the main A30 road and the small harbour.

John Vaughan

Plate 235: Close up study of *Conqueror* at Penzance. The class 50 bogies are virtually identical to those on its English Electric class 37 and class 55 stablemates as are the traction motors. Behind the louvres are the massive radiators to cool the V16 engine. Beneath the nameplate is the main 1000 gallon fuel tank.

John Vaughan

CLASS 50 SPECIFICATION

Weight in working order 115 tonnes
Weight ex works 111 tonnes
Wheel arrangement Co — Co
Engine — English Electric 16 CSVT
Power Output — 2700 hp at 850 rpm
Length over buffers 68' 6''

Plate 238: The 16 cylinder English Electric 16 CSVT diesel engine which produces 2700 hp at 850 rpm.
courtesy G.E.C. Traction Ltd.

Initially the class 50s were overhauled at Crewe Works but the work was later transferred to Doncaster, where they handle class 37s and 55s both of which have similar parts (especially bogies and traction motors) to the 50s. Laira depot at Plymouth has the facilities to cope with all aspects of maintenance except where the entire diesel engine needs to be removed from the locomotive. On average a class 50 will go to works for a major overhaul about every four years.

Plate 239: A class 50 bogie from No. 50 042 at Doncaster works.
Colin Marsden

Overall width 9' 1¼''
Overall height 12' 11¾''
Total wheelbase 56' 2''
Tractive Effort (maximum) 48,500 lb
Tractive Effort (continuous) 33,000 lb
Tractive motors — English Electric type 538/5A
Wheel bearings — Timken roller
Fuel Capacity — 1055 imperial gallons
Maximum service speed — 100 mph
Train heating — electric
Built — Vulcan Foundry
Wheel diameter — 3' 7''

Appendix 2

DRIVER'S CONTROLS —
ENGLISH ELECTRIC CLASS 50

1 AWS Indicator
2 AWS Reset switch
3 Train brake
4 Air brake
5 Bogie straight air brake
6 Air brake pipe gauge
7 Vacuum brake gauge
8 Speedometer
9 Windscreen wiper
10 Windscreen washer
11 Warning horn
12 Panel light switch
13 Wheel slip brake button
14 Power handle
15 Forward/reverse master switch
16 Wheel slip warning light
17 Overload reset
18 Engine start button
19 Current limit setting
20 Amps output

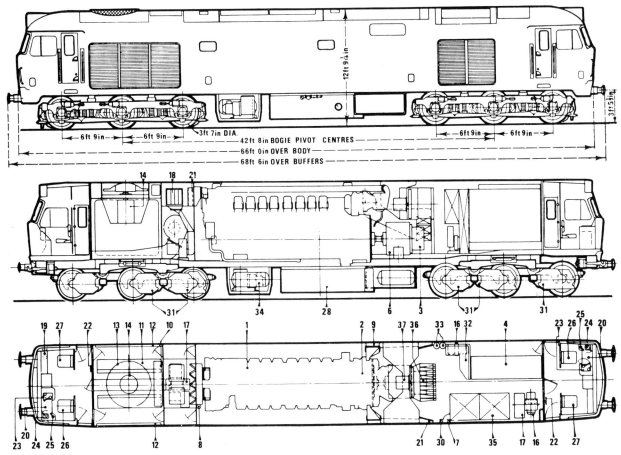

1. Engine 16 CSVT
2. Main generator EE 840
3. Auxiliary generator E 911
4. Main equipment frame
5. Batteries
6. Train heating generator
7. Urinal
8. Engine fuel supply unit
9. Engine air ducting
10. Radiator header tank
11. Radiators
12. Radiator shutters
13. Radiator fan

14. Radiator fan motor
15. Compressor WTG 3VC75
16. Exhausters
17. Traction motor blowers
18. Air filters
19. Sand fillers
20. Driver's desk
21. Air filters
22. Handbrake
23. Master controller
24. Automatic air brake valve
25. Independent air brake valve
26. Driver's seat

27. Assistant's seat
28. Main 1,000-gal fuel tank
29. Main fuel tank gauge
30. Urinal flush tank
31. Traction motors EE 538
32. Brake equipment
33. CO$_2$ bottles
34. Air reservoirs
35. Dynamic brake
36. Air filter (equipment compartment)
37. Fan motor

Appendix 3

THE CLASS 50 FLEET — FACTS AND FIGURES

Present BR fleet number	Vulcan Works number	Date of manufacture	Fleet number as delivered	Name	Date named
50 001 *	D1143	1967	D401	*Dreadnought*	10.4.78
50 002 *	D1142	1967	D402	*Superb*	21.3.78
50 003	D1144	1967	D403	*Temeraire*	9.5.78
50 004	D1145	1967	D404	*St Vincent*	9.5.78
50 005	D1146	1967	D405	*Collingwood*	5.4.78
50 006	D1147	1967	D406	*Neptune*	—
50 007	D1148	1967	D407	*Hercules*	6.4.78
50 008	D1149	1967	D408	*Thunderer*	1.9.78
50 009	D1150	1967	D409	*Conqueror*	8.5.78
50 010	D1151	1967	D410	*Monarch*	16.3.78
50 011	D1152	1967	D411	*Centurion*	—
50 012	D1153	1967	D412	*Benbow*	3.4.78
50 013	D1154	1967	D413	*Agincourt*	19.4.78
50 014	D1155	1967	D414	*Warspite*	30.5.78
50 015	D1156	1967	D415	*Valiant*	21.4.78
50 016	D1157	1967	D416	*Barham*	3.4.78
50 017	D1158	1967	D417	*Royal Oak*	24.4.78
50 018	D1159	1967	D418	*Resolution*	6.4.78
50 019	D1160	1967	D419	*Ramilles*	18.4.78
50 020	D1161	1968	D420	*Revenge*	7.7.78
50 021	D1162	1968	D421	*Rodney*	31.7.78
50 022	D1163	1968	D422	*Anson*	20.4.78
50 023	D1164	1968	D423	*Howe*	17.5.78
50 024	D1165	1968	D424	*Vanguard*	15.5.78
50 025	D1166	1968	D425	*Invincible*	6.6.78
50 026	D1167	1968	D426	*Indomitable*	29.3.78
50 027	D1168	1968	D427	*Lion*	17.4.78
50 028	D1169	1968	D428	*Tiger*	10.5.78
50 029	D1170	1968	D429	*Renown*	26.10.78
50 030	D1171	1968	D430	*Repulse*	10.4.78
50 031	D1172	1968	D431	*Hood*	28.6.78
50 032	D1173	1968	D432	*Courageous*	7.7.78
50 033	D1174	1968	D433	*Glorious*	26.6.78
50 034	D1175	1968	D434	*Furious*	6.4.78
50 035	D1176	1968	D435	*Ark Royal*	17.1.78
50 036	D1177	1968	D436	*Victorious*	16.5.78
50 037	D1178	1968	437	*Illustrious*	8.6.78
50 038	D1179	1968	438	*Formidable*	5.5.78
50 039	D1180	1968	439	*Implacable*	20.6.78
50 040	D1181	1968	440	*Leviathan*	15.9.78
50 041	D1182	1968	441	*Bulwark*	8.5.78
50 042	D1183	1968	442	*Triumph*	4.10.78
50 043	D1184	1968	443	*Eagle*	28.6.78
50 044	D1185	1968	444	*Exeter*	26.4.78
50 045	D1186	1968	445	*Achilles*	12.4.78
50 046	D1187	1968	446	*Ajax*	11.10.78
50 047	D1188	1968	447	*Swiftsure*	26.5.78
50 048	D1189	1968	448	*Dauntless*	16.3.78
50 049	D1190	1968	449	*Defiance*	2.5.78
50 050	D1141	1967	D400	*Fearless*	+ 4.8.78

+ nameplate removed 7.8.78 — officially renamed 23.8.78
— not named at the time of going to press
* 50 002 was built before 50 001